5/98

Searching for
Velociraptor

Searching for *Velociraptor*

Lowell Dingus
and Mark A. Norell

HarperCollins*Publishers*

The Gobi Desert, 1990

We drove through the desolate desert valleys and jagged mountains of southern Mongolia, searching for dinosaurs. We peered through binoculars looking for cliffs of sandstone. That was where we thought we'd find our prey—*Velociraptor*. Hidden in this stark and beautiful landscape were the fossilized secrets of dinosaurs that lived about 72 million years ago. We intended to discover them.

So much time and planning had gone into this expedition, it was hard to believe we were really here. Even harder to believe was that five such expeditions were mounted by the American Museum of Natural History between 1922 and 1930. The famous explorer and naturalist Roy Chapman Andrews had set out looking for fossils of early humans, but ended up discovering the first well-documented eggs of dinosaurs, a new primitive horned dinosaur called *Protoceratops*, and a new carnivorous dinosaur called *Velociraptor*.

Andrews' discoveries were now legendary. Never in our wildest dreams had we imagined that we would follow in his footsteps. But in 1990 scientists from the Mongolian Academy of Sciences asked our Museum if we would like to return to the fossil fields that Andrews had made famous. Would we?! Along with several other paleontologists from the Museum, we immediately accepted.

That had been months ago, and now here we were at last. Searching for *Velociraptor*. Hoping to make a great find. Hoping to shed new light on how birds evolved from dinosaurs. These outcroppings of sandstone might hold the answers to the secrets of evolution we had wanted to know all our lives.

left: *the spectacular badlands at Khermeen Tsav*

top: *Roy Chapman Andrews leading the Museum's expedition to the Gobi Desert in the 1920s*

above: *seeking directions with our Mongolian co-workers*

Making Plans

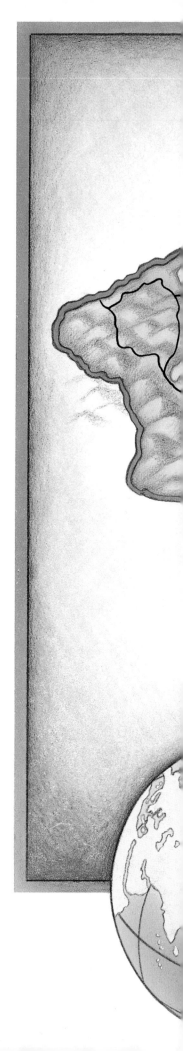

In the 1920s organizing an expedition to Asia took years of planning and fund-raising. Seventy years later it wasn't much easier. It was incredible how much time and money it took to mobilize a team of six paleontologists and geologists, one photographer, and one newspaper reporter for a trip halfway around the world.

Probably most important were the agreements that had to be written between the Museum, the Mongolian Academy of Sciences, and the government of Mongolia setting out where the fossils would be collected, studied, and kept. It was agreed that we could take the fossils we found back to our Museum to study them, but that all the specimens would eventually be returned to the national museum in Mongolia.

With that settled, we could start to pack in earnest. Since we'd never worked in Mongolia before, we didn't know what to take. The Mongolian paleontologists were very helpful with this. It was also fortunate that some of them knew English well enough to act as translators. As field equipment, cans and packages of freeze-dried food, medical supplies, etc., began to pile up, we shipped them by boat and then train from the United States, through China, and on to Mongolia. We even shipped four-wheel-drive vehicles to help us move across the rugged terrain.

After several months of shopping and shipping, we were all very anxious to start searching— *Velociraptor* awaited, or so we hoped.

RUSSIA

N

MONGOLIA

1

2

GOBI DESERT

8

3

10

5

9 7 6

4

CHINA

ASIA

OUR 1991 ROUTE

1. Ulaan Baatar   6. Khulsan
2. Saynshand   7. Naran Bulag
3. Khara Khutul   8. Altan Ula
4. Dalangadazad   9. Khermeen Tsav
5. Flaming Cliffs   10. Tugrigeen

Setting Forth

It took nearly twenty-four hours to fly from New York via Tokyo, then Beijing, to the capital of Mongolia, Ulaan Baator. Finally, after several days spent organizing our equipment and checking to make sure we had all the right governmental permits, we were ready to leave for the Gobi Desert.

There were no good maps for where we wanted to go. Some of our Mongolian colleagues had been to the fossil sites we would visit, so they could act as guides, but we also carried small navigational computers that could receive directional signals from satellites.

It took three days to drive south from Ulaan Baatar across the grassy steppes to the closest place we could find fossils—the Flaming Cliffs where the

plotting a course

Andrews crew had discovered the first dinosaur eggs.

Over the next five weeks we drove hundreds of miles to ten different localities scattered along the border between Mongolia and the People's Republic of China. We made our way through rugged mountain canyons and across or around dangerous dune fields. We bounced up and down dry streambeds, but even with our four-wheel-drive vehicles, we often got stuck in the soft sand and gravel. Occasionally we could travel the dirt roads linking the small desert towns. No more than a few hundred people lived in any of these villages, but to us they were a lifeline; in them we might be able to buy some bread, rice, and gasoline.

At each stop we set up a camp and stayed for several days. Water came from the nearest well, which was often a several-hours' drive away. There was no electricity—the only light at night came from our flashlights. Most nights we slept out under starlit skies.

above: *a small Mongolian village deep in the desert*

top left: *a typical campsite in the Gobi Desert*

The Treasure Hunt

Previous expeditions had identified many good places to begin our search by locating cliffs and ridges of red or white sandstone, where fossils are often found. We discovered even more localities using satellite photos, on which sandstone outcrops are clearly visible. All these sites became a sort of treasure map to guide us through the desert.

But what a grueling treasure hunt it could be! Each paleontologist spent long hours walking over hills, along cliffs, and across streambeds staring at the ground, hoping to see pieces of bone or teeth eroding out of the sandstone. Our eyes are our most important tools. If you lose your concentration and don't look carefully enough, you can walk right by a spectacular fossil.

Since visibility was crucial, our days were ruled by the sun. We'd head out about eight thirty A.M. and not return to camp until six or seven P.M., when the light faded. Typically, the sandstone outcrops we were searching extended across several square miles, so we would often split up in order to explore as much of the area as possible.

We call this part of the collecting process prospecting, because it is similar to the way prospectors search for gold. Prospecting can be exhausting, especially when the sun and blowing sand have worn you out and you are just not finding many fossils. And during the first few weeks of our expedition, we weren't finding many interesting fossils at all.

At the Flaming Cliffs, we did find one spectacular skeleton of the armored dinosaur *Saichania.* We also collected more than fifty well-preserved skulls of small lizards and primitive mammals. All these fossils have provided us with important scientific information, but the big find we'd all hoped for remained elusive.

left: *searching the Flaming Cliffs*

top: *taking a closer look at a fragment of bone on the surface*

middle: *a small skull*

above: *digging deeper to see if more of a skeleton is buried under the surface*

11

Velociraptor!

After four frustrating weeks, we arrived at our last site, Tugrigeen Shireh. Time was running out. We couldn't miss our flight out of Mongolia, because very few flights took off at all. As our days dwindled down to one, we began to lose hope of making a big find.

But on our last day, at the end of the afternoon, one of the paleontologists from the Museum began his hike back to camp and decided to prospect down a broad ravine. Walking slowly across the rocks, he noticed some pieces of grayish-white bone lying in a small bed of soft sand. Kneeling down to get a closer look, he could see some sharp, curved teeth sticking out of the bones. A wave of excitement washed over him. From the shape of the teeth, he knew immediately that he'd found what we were looking for—*Velociraptor*!

Several pieces of the skull and lower jaw were just sitting on the sand, having been eroded out of the rock by year after year of constant wind and occasional rain. He knew there was a good chance that more of the skeleton still lay buried in the sandstone below and that he'd need help and more equipment to dig it out. So, after marking the site with small piles of rocks, he hurried back to camp. As he approached, his excitement was obvious, and after he'd told us what he'd found, four of us rushed out to see for ourselves. The long weeks of walking had finally paid off . . . in the last hours of the last day of our expedition.

the sandstone ravine where our Velociraptor *was found*

inset: *the bones and teeth of the snout as they were found sitting on the sand*

Digging Up the Skeleton

When the four of us got to our *Velociraptor*, it was nearing sunset. Because we had to leave the next morning, we knew we had to work quickly, but also very carefully. Our *Velociraptor* skeleton, like most fossils, was extremely fragile. Even though the fossil was made of hard minerals that had replaced most of the original bone, after millions of years of being buried and then eroded, the bones and teeth were badly fractured.

Our first task was to find out how much of the skeleton had been preserved. We squirted a special glue called Butvar onto the loose pieces to harden them before we gingerly wrapped them in tissue paper for protection. Then, using small paintbrushes, we gently cleared the sand off the bones still visible on the surface. From the size of the skull, we knew that the whole skeleton would be about 4 to 5 feet long from the end of its snout to the tip of its tail. However, we didn't know if it had all been preserved or in what position the body had been buried. To find out, we would have to uncover the bones leading back from the skull one by one. Once the loose sand had been brushed away, small awls were used to carefully scrape the harder sandstone off the tops of the bones that were still buried. At last we could see our *Velociraptor* take shape.

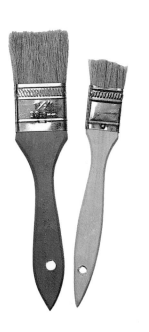

collecting tools

top: *the fossil as it was found*

middle: *brushing away the sand, looking for buried pieces of bone*

bottom: *the partially exposed skeleton; the roof of the skull is seen in the middle of the block, and the neck vertebrae extend up toward the top of the picture*

15

Protecting the Broken Bones

When the skeleton was partially exposed, we dug a trench around it so that the bones were sitting on top of a small island of sandstone. But before we could dig the skeleton completely out of the ground, we needed to make a plaster cast to hold the skeleton together and protect it during the trip back to the Museum. First we applied a layer of tissue paper to the sandy surface where the bone was exposed. The tissue would keep the plaster from sticking to the fossil and damaging it. Next we cut strips of plaster bandages, soaked them in water, and layered them over the tissue. This created a protective cast just like one a doctor would use around a broken bone.

After the bandaging was finished, we took a break for about twenty minutes while the plaster dried and hardened. It had taken us only an hour to excavate the fossil to this point, but the sunlight was fading and we were anxious to finish the job.

Finally, the plaster cast was set. Using a rock hammer, we dug underneath the block. Now we were ready for the moment of truth. It was time to roll the block over and hope that the sandstone and fossils would not fall out of the plaster cast. Fortunately, the block held together, and all that was left to do was plaster up the bottom side. Soon we were on our way back to camp with our 40-pound trophy. Now it was time to celebrate! We would be going home with a prize after all.

top & middle: *digging the trench around the delicate fossils*

bottom: *applying a layer of tissue on top of the exposed fossil bones*

top: *the nearly completed plaster jacket*

middle: *an initial coating of bandages is placed on top of the tissue*

bottom: *waiting for the plaster cast to harden*

Back at the Museum

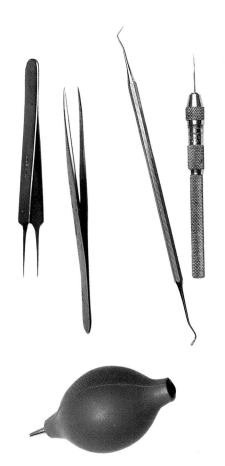

After wrapping the plaster block in foam rubber padding, we packed it snugly in a wooden crate for shipment by plane to New York.

We made it back to New York before our fossil and had to wait agonizing weeks for it to arrive. When it finally did come, we all gathered around to open the box and see if our prize had survived the journey. What a relief when we saw it had come through without being damaged!

Now we could begin removing the fossil from the rock: a process called preparation. Preparation must be done before the fossil can be studied or displayed, so it was one of the most critical steps in our *Velociraptor*'s evolution.

Preparators are highly skilled technicians who patiently remove rock from around fossil bones. They began by cutting away part of the plaster jacket. Then, using a combination of small brushes and picks (the same kinds that your dentist uses), they began to delicately remove the sandstone. As they uncovered the specimen, the preparators would coat each fossil bone with glue to harden it. Even with these precautions, though, small fragments of fossilized bone often broke off and had to be glued back on.

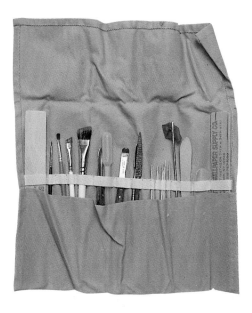

Because the fossils are so delicate, much of the preparation must be done under a microscope. Careful notes and photographs are taken along the way, so that long after the surrounding rock is removed, scientists will be able to see how the specimen was found.

Finally, after many hundreds of hours of painstaking work, the hundreds of pieces of *Velociraptor* bone were freed from their sandstone casing. And after all those pieces were fitted together again, the specimen would be ready for study.

left: *preparator at work in the Museum's laboratory*

above: *preparator's tools*

19

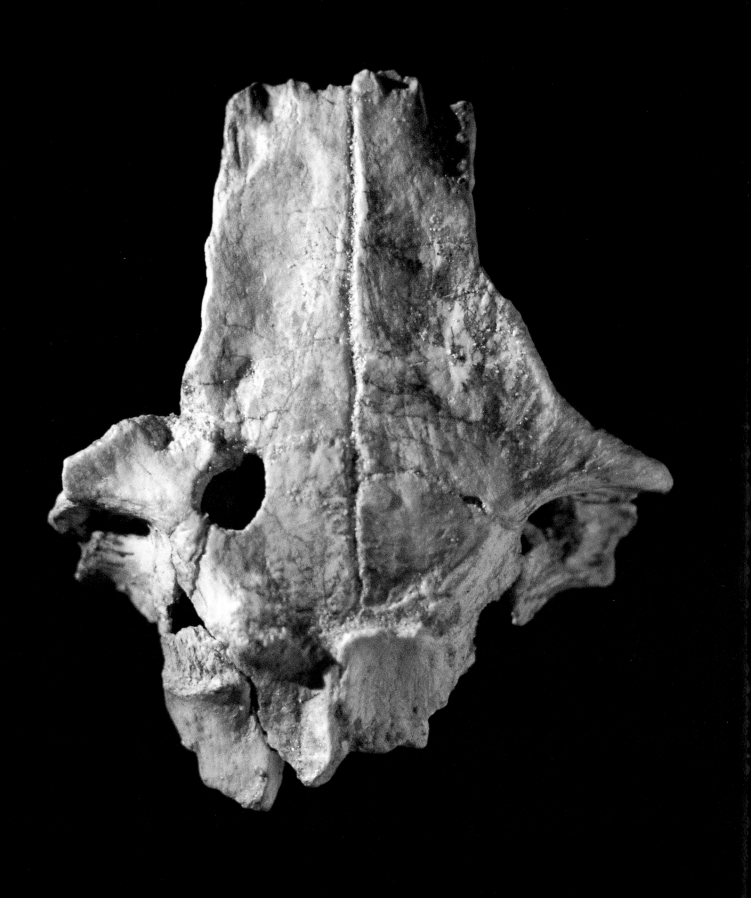

What the Bones Tell Us

By studying the *Velociraptor* bones, we have learned many things about how this animal lived and died. Our find was not a complete skeleton—most of the hind legs, tail, and hips of our dinosaur were missing. But because all the bones of the skull were tightly interlocked along their edges, we knew that our *Velociraptor* was an old adult when it died. In younger animals, the bones do not interlock so tightly.

The fact that so many bones were missing suggests that scavengers may have fed on the carcass after the *Velociraptor* died. We found some possible corroboration for this theory in the skull. We were amazed to find a line of holes on the top of the skull between the eyes, in the bone that covers the front part of the brain. These holes exactly matched the jaw size and bite pattern of a *Velociraptor*. This evidence tells us that our dinosaur was bitten across the head by a similar animal—very possibly another *Velociraptor*. Perhaps two animals were fighting for territory or mates. Or maybe our *Velociraptor* was the victim of a hunt. We can't tell. It's possible the *Velociraptor* had already died from other causes before the bite. But it is also possible that the bite is what killed it. Such a bite would surely have been lethal, because the teeth would have severely damaged the brain.

left: *top view of our* Velociraptor's *skull; the large round hole on the left side and the smaller hole beneath it are puncture wounds where another animal bit through the top of our* Velociraptor's *skull*

below: Velociraptor *skull, side view*

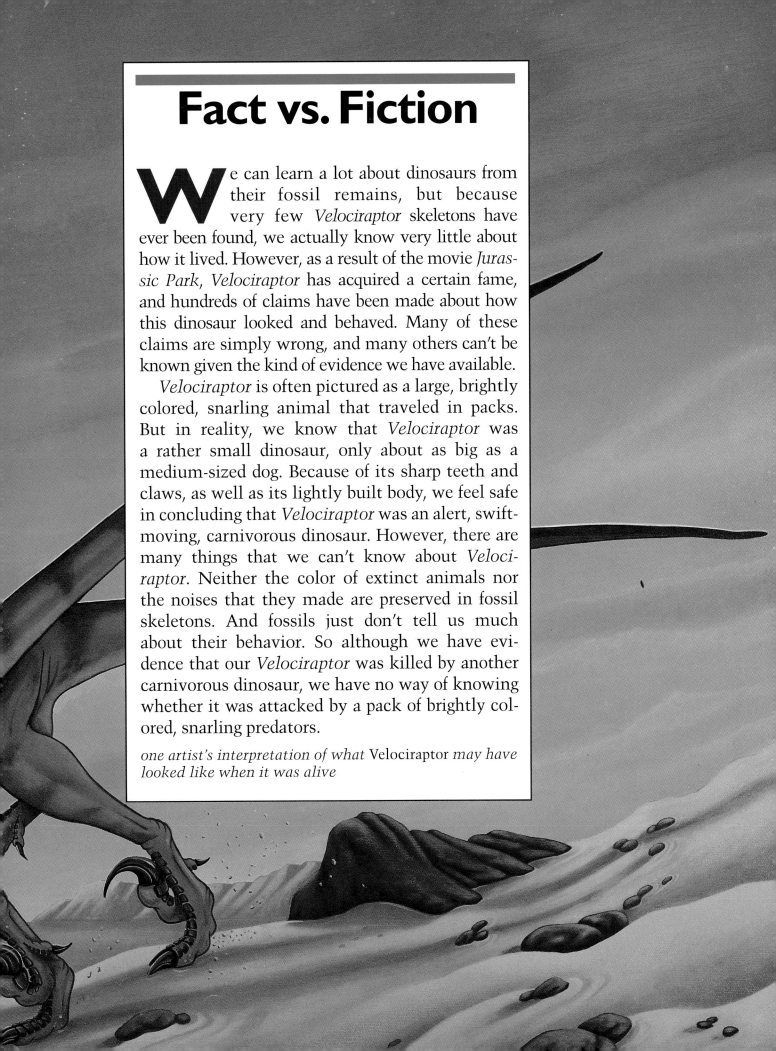

Fact vs. Fiction

We can learn a lot about dinosaurs from their fossil remains, but because very few *Velociraptor* skeletons have ever been found, we actually know very little about how it lived. However, as a result of the movie *Jurassic Park*, *Velociraptor* has acquired a certain fame, and hundreds of claims have been made about how this dinosaur looked and behaved. Many of these claims are simply wrong, and many others can't be known given the kind of evidence we have available.

Velociraptor is often pictured as a large, brightly colored, snarling animal that traveled in packs. But in reality, we know that *Velociraptor* was a rather small dinosaur, only about as big as a medium-sized dog. Because of its sharp teeth and claws, as well as its lightly built body, we feel safe in concluding that *Velociraptor* was an alert, swift-moving, carnivorous dinosaur. However, there are many things that we can't know about *Velociraptor*. Neither the color of extinct animals nor the noises that they made are preserved in fossil skeletons. And fossils just don't tell us much about their behavior. So although we have evidence that our *Velociraptor* was killed by another carnivorous dinosaur, we have no way of knowing whether it was attacked by a pack of brightly colored, snarling predators.

one artist's interpretation of what Velociraptor *may have looked like when it was alive*

Why *Velociraptor* Is Important

Because even the best fossils of *Velociraptor* don't tell us everything we'd like to know, we have to find other evidence to help us make educated guesses about this dinosaur. We can hope to learn how *Velociraptor* behaved by looking at its closest living relatives. To decide which animals are close evolutionary relatives, we search for living animals that share skeletal characteristics with *Velociraptor*. Just as you resemble other members of your family, animals that share many characteristics are closely related.

Extensive searches have revealed that birds and crocodiles both share many characteristics with *Velociraptor*. All three have an opening in the side of the lower jaw (1). Also, their legs are built to be held fairly straight up and down underneath the body when these animals run. As we look more closely at the skeletons, we see that *Velociraptor* shares even more characteristics with birds. *Velociraptor* and birds both have feet with large forward-pointing toes and one small one that points backward (2). Each also has an S-shaped neck (3). Even the long arm and wrist bones in *Velociraptor* are very similar to the bones in bird wings (4).

Because it is so closely related to both birds and crocodiles, we can guess that *Velociraptor* had most of the characteristics shared by birds and crocodiles. For example, it probably saw in color, built nests, and took care of its young, just as living birds and crocodiles do. And because *Velociraptor* is more closely related to birds, it may have also had characteristics found in birds, such as warm-bloodedness. But at this time we cannot be sure.

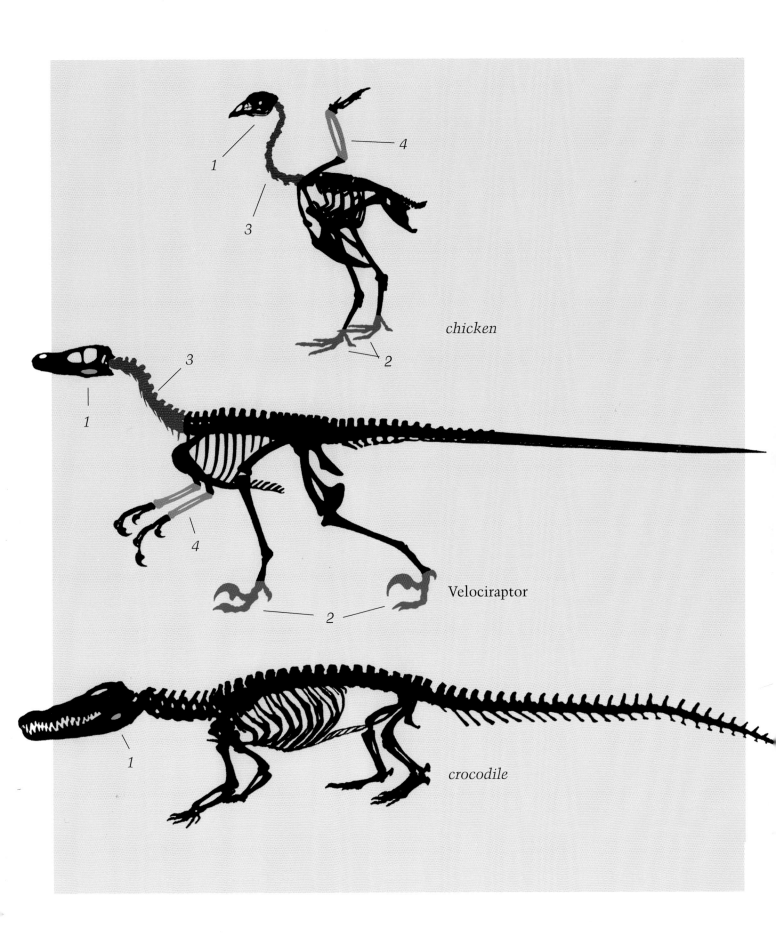

chicken

Velociraptor

crocodile

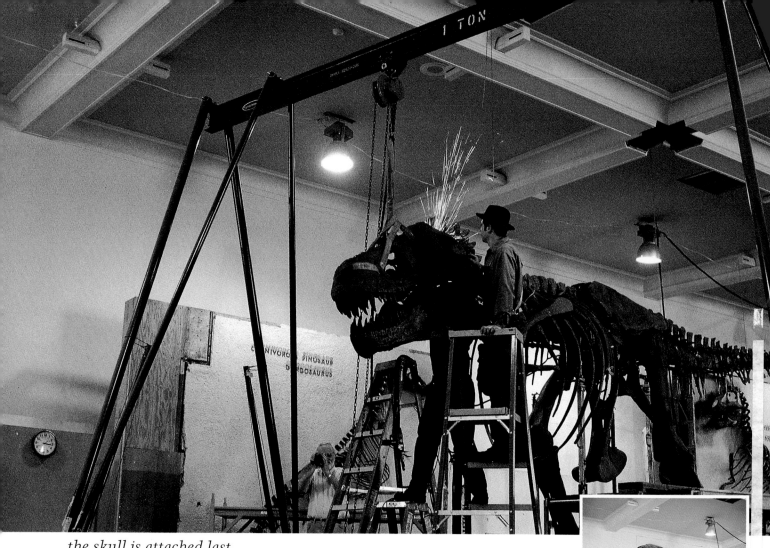

the skull is attached last

framing the hip bones

welding the toes

the legs and hips are set

adding the neck in pieces

nearly complete

Mounting a Skeleton

Once a fossil has been prepared and studied, it is often mounted to be put on display in a museum. Our *Velociraptor* skeleton couldn't be mounted, as we had to return it to Mongolia. It was also missing so many bones that it would not make a great display. But the American Museum of Natural History had a wonderful skeleton ready for display, so while we were waiting for our *Velociraptor* to be prepared, we helped to develop plans to build a mounted skeleton of *Tyrannosaurus* for the new fossil halls.

Like fossil preparators, mount makers are very talented technicians. Their job is to plan and then build the metal framework that holds up the fossil skeleton. Most are experts in both anatomy and metal sculpting.

They began by creating a series of drawings showing several possible positions. Then, together, we decided which pose to choose.

Thick rods of steel were heated and bent to run under the backbone and down the backs of the legs. Smaller rods were bent to support the long arms and the hands. Tiny pieces of metal were bent and welded onto the larger rods to form hooks to hold the individual bones securely. Then all the pieces of the metal framework were either screwed or welded together. The result is a dramatic image of what the dinosaur might have looked liked.

mount maker's tools

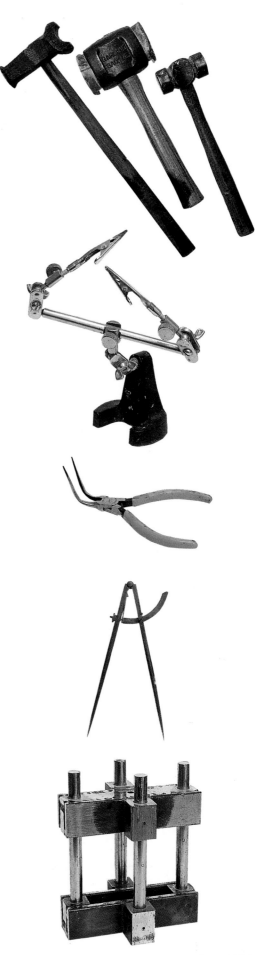

A Journey's End

This is the end of a fossil's journey—from the field where it was discovered and collected to the laboratory where it was prepared and studied, then to the exhibition hall where it stands mounted for all the world to see. But even as people crowd the Museum to share what we have learned, our journey will continue. We will return to Mongolia and other fossil treasure grounds again and again. Every step we have taken has taught us more about the history of life on Earth, and we hope that every future step will make that story more complete.

Hall of Saurischian Dinosaurs

Where You Can Find Dinosaurs

The American Museum of Natural History (Central Park West at 79th Street in New York City) has the world's largest and most representative collection and exhibition of dinosaurs. Some other large dinosaur exhibitions can be found at:

The Academy of Natural Sciences
19th and the Parkway
Logan Square
Philadelphia, Pennsylvania 19103

Carnegie Museum of Natural History
4400 Forbes Avenue
Pittsburgh, Pennsylvania 15213

Denver Museum of Natural History
City Park
Denver, Colorado 80205

Dinosaur National Monument
P.O. Box 128
Jensen, Utah 84035

Field Museum of Natural History
Roosevelt Road at Lake Shore Drive
Chicago, Illinois 60605

Los Angeles County Museum
900 Exposition Boulevard
Los Angeles, California 90007

Museum of Comparative Zoology
Harvard University
Cambridge, Massachusetts 02138

National Museum of Natural History
Smithsonian Institution
Washington, D.C. 20560

Peabody Museum of Natural History
Yale University
170 Whitney Avenue
New Haven, Connecticut 06511

University of Wyoming
Geological Museum
Box 3254
Laramie, Wyoming 82071

Utah Museum of Natural History
University of Utah
Salt Lake City, Utah 84112

National Museum of Natural Sciences
P.O. Box 3443
Station D
Ottawa, Ontario K1P64P
Canada

Royal Ontario Museum
100 Queen's Park
Toronto, Ontario M5S2C6
Canada

Tyrrell Museum of Paleontology
P.O. Box 7500
Drumheller, Alberta T0J0Y0
Canada

Museo Argentino de Ciencias Naturales
Av. Angel Gallardo 470
1405 Buenos Aires
Argentina

Hall of Ornithischian Dinosaurs

Lowell Dingus, Ph.D., is a dinosaur paleontologist who has traveled to such inhospitable locales as the Gobi Desert badlands in Mongolia and the Hell Creek and Tullock Formations in Montana in his search for fossils. He is affiliated with the American Museum of Natural History in New York City, which has the largest collection of dinosaur and other fossil vertebrates in the world. Most recently, Dr. Dingus served as the Director of the Museum's stunning Fossil Hall Renovation.

Mark A. Norell, Ph.D., is also affiliated with the American Museum of Natural History. He is both the Associate Curator of the Department of Vertebrate Paleontology and a Curator for the Halls of Dinosaurs and Hall of Vertebrate Origins. He too has spent many years traveling the world in search of fossils. In the past ten years he has been the leader or coleader on international expeditions in Chilean Patagonia, the central Chilean Andes, the West African Sahel, Mongolia, and Cuba.

PHOTO CREDITS: *pages 2–3, 4, 12–13, 15, 16, 17, Lowell Dingus; page 5 top, American Museum of Natural History; pages 5 bottom, 8–9, 10–11, 32, Fred Conrad; pages 6-7, Deborah Maze; pages 14, 18, 19, 20, 21, 25, 27, Mick Ellison; pages 22–23, Ed Heck; page 26 top and middle left, Denis Finnin; page 26 middle right and center, bottom left and right, Phil Fraley; pages 28–29, 30, Scott Frances.*

Searching for *Velociraptor*

Library of Congress Cataloging-in-Publication Data
Dingus, Lowell.
  Searching for Velociraptor / Lowell Dingus and Mark A. Norell.
    p.   cm.
  Summary: An account of the search for, recovery, preservation, and study of the fossilized remains of the dinosaur Velociraptor as narrated by two paleontologists who led the expedition to Mongolia.
    ISBN 0-06-025893-4. — ISBN 0-06-025894-2 (lib. bdg.)
    1. Velociraptor—Juvenile literature. [1. Velociraptor.   2. Dinosaurs.
3. Paleontology.]   I. Norell, Mark.   II. Title.
QE862.S3D56   1996   95-22238
567.9'7—dc20   CIP
                                                                       AC

   2   3   4   5   6   7   8   9   10
❖
First Edition